JAY
PAYLEITNER

LIFE◉L◉GY

THINGS YOU CAN COUNT ON BESIDES YOUR FINGERS

BroadStreet
PUBLISHING

BroadStreet Publishing Group, LLC
Racine, Wisconsin, USA
BroadStreetPublishing.com

LIFEOLOGY: THINGS YOU CAN COUNT ON BESIDES YOUR FINGERS

ISBN-13: 978-1-4245-5265-8 (hardcover)
ISBN-13: 978-1-4245-5266-5 (e-book)

Stock or custom editions of BroadStreet Publishing titles may be purchased in bulk for educational, business, ministry, fundraising, or sales promotional use. For information, please e-mail info@ broadstreetpublishing.com.

Cover by Chris Garborg at garborgdesign.com
Interior by Katherine Lloyd at theDESKonline.com

Printed in China
16 17 18 19 20 5 4 3 2 1

CONTENTS

INTRODUCTION

This is not a book of famous quotations from famous people. You won't find any witticisms from Abe Lincoln, Mark Twain, or Oscar Wilde.

What you will find are Lifeology truths you can actually use. More than 750 words of wisdom learned the hard way, stumbled over, heard in passing, or generated out of thin air.

These precepts have been gathered for one purpose: to be shared. So use them. Tweet them. Pin them. Post them. If it feels right, shove your favorite Lifeology truism down the throat of your most annoying adversary. After all, sometimes the truth hurts.

Actually, the best use of this book might be to equip you to rise majestically above your friends and foes. It's a beautiful thing to have just the right thing to say at just the right time.

For your convenience, we've divided *Lifeology* into more than two dozen surprising and eclectic categories. You are allowed to have a favorite category, but don't miss the others. In two categories, we identify an undeniable source—William Shakespeare and the Bible. The words of the bard and the Creator of the universe, respectively, were just too invaluable to pass up.

But what about the other categories? Who was the first to grunt or speak the other Lifeology truths? Who was the first to chisel them in stone, scribble them on a yellow pad, or clack them out on a typewriter, laptop, or iPad? In quite a few cases, it was the author of this book. In many others, the phrase can only be attributed to some anonymous, incognito individual. Or maybe we should simply give credit to the collective genius of the universe.

As you read, if you believe you can identify a specific writer or speaker who first delivered any of these truths, track us down at lifeologybook.com. We want to give credit where credit is due.

In any case, keep this book handy. When you feel overwhelmed and surrounded by ignoramuses, numbskulls, and the ill-informed, know that you have hundreds of trustworthy truths at your fingertips—ready to apply to life.

Welcome to the mind-expanding world of *Lifeology*.

RELATIONSHIP LIFEOLOGY

People are more important than things.

A friend is one who walks in
when the rest of the world walks out.

He who throws mud loses ground.

Make friends before you need them.

If you don't believe in yourself,
neither will anyone else.

People don't care how much you know,
until they know how much you care.

Courtesy is free.

If you hold something against someone, there's a good chance they're holding something against you.

A bad temper gets you into trouble. Pride keeps you there.

Marriage is the most expensive way to get your laundry done for free.

Love means dying to self.

Whatever a bride does in the weeks leading up to her wedding cannot be held against her.

Tough times reveal true friends.

A man is known by the company he avoids.

The fastest way to receive love is to give love.

It takes two to tangle.

Character is what you are.
Reputation is what people think you are.

The way you perceive yourself
is the primary influence on the way
other people perceive you.

Liars and cheaters believe
everyone lies and cheats.

Speak selectively.
Tell everyone everything and there's no reason
for anyone to engage you again.

Teams get more done
when no one cares who gets the credit.

Guilt is the gift that keeps on giving.

Talent is God given. Be humble.

Fame is man given. Be careful.

Let them lean on you now, and you won't
have to pick them up off the floor later.

A man's wife is as beautiful as he sees her.

Relationships work when two people
are ready to sacrifice anything and
everything for one another.

Laughter is the shortest distance
between two people.

A friend is someone who knows the song
in your heart and can sing it back to you
when you have forgotten the words.

Love isn't the person you can see yourself with,
it's the person you can't see yourself without.

Who gossips to you will gossip about you.

Just because you said it
doesn't mean they heard it.

If you don't listen, you're not communicating.

If you lend someone twenty bucks
and never see that person again,
consider it twenty bucks well spent.

PRACTICAL LIFEOLOGY

Don't eat yellow snow.

Don't mess with people who serve your food.

Just because you can, doesn't mean you should.

You can do it right or make time to do it over.

When you finally get your household
budget together, there is an
overwhelming sense of relief.

If you find yourself in a hole,
the first thing to do is stop digging.

The quickest way to find something you've lost
is to buy a replacement.

You never forget something
learned the hard way.

The only sure way to double your money
is to fold it over
and put it back in your pocket.

Keep your eyes and ears open.

Your life can't go according to plan
if you have no plan.

The most satisfied diners
have made friends with the chef.

If you eat the last cookie,
throw away the package.

PRACTICAL LIFEOLOGY

If you put all your eggs in one basket,
guard that basket.

With the right motivation,
old dogs can learn new tricks.

To get a loan
you must first prove you don't need it.

Whatever hits the fan
will not be evenly distributed.

Christianity is not being a better person,
it's being a new person.

Whatever you subsidize,
you get more of.

The best time to plant a tree is twenty years ago.
The second best time is now.

Goals not written down are mere wishes.

Never fry bacon in the nude.

You get what you give.

You can lead a horse to water
but you can't make him drink.

You can lead a man to knowledge
but you can't make him think.

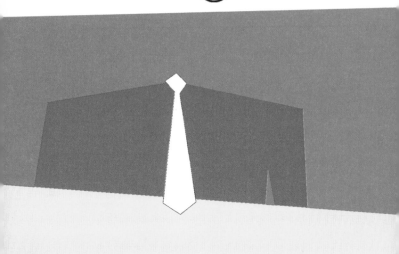

DO-GREAT-THINGS
LIFEOLOGY

The road to success has many detours,
roadblocks, and parking spaces.

Keep your eyes on the prize.

There are only two ways to get from
point A to Point B—find one or make one.

**What makes you different
is what makes you great.**

You have to think you can before you can.

**You will not find a solution
by dwelling on the problem.**

You never really find your wings
until you take the leap.

Proceed as if success is inevitable.

The only real limits
are the ones you put on yourself.

Follow the crowd
and you will never be followed by a crowd.

Success depends on big plans
and small choices.

Just over the hill of your greatest discouragements
are your greatest achievements.

To reach a great height
a person needs to have great depth.

You can wait on the beach
for your ship to come in
or you can swim out to it.

**The whole world steps aside for the man
who knows where he is going.**

Greatness requires patience.

**No one ever found an answer
by looking for excuses.**

The person who really wants to do something
finds a way, the other finds an excuse.

The road to success is always under construction.

Success comes in cans, not in cannots.

Don't let what you can't do
interfere with what you can do.

There are no shortcuts to any place worth going.

Avoid traffic jams by going the extra mile.

Success begets success.

How you deal with failure
determines your success.

The meaning of life is to find your gift.

Write a thousand words a day,
four days a week, and in four months
you'll have the first draft of your first book.

DO-GREAT-THINGS LIFEOLOGY

Blazing new trails leads to new discoveries.

It takes vision and creativity
to discover something new
on a well-worn path.

You are what you do,
not what you say you'll do.

Never say never.

If you start that thing today that requires a year of your
life, it will be done next year. If you don't start that thing
that requires a year of your life, twelve months from now
it will still be next year and that thing still won't be done.

Applause should never be the goal.

Life is tragic for those who have plenty to live on
and nothing to live for.

Big things often have small beginnings.

You can avoid criticism by doing nothing,
saying nothing, and being nothing.

Turn a loss to a win by looking for the lesson.

Make no small plans but keep
listening to see if God has an even better plan.

Success is the ability
to turn a negative into a positive.

If you don't try, you cannot succeed.

Life sometimes requires you to do
what you cannot do.

OFFHAND
LIFEOLOGY

When your mind wanders,
maybe you should follow it.

One reason people do not like most photos
of themselves is because they're most familiar
with the reverse image they see in a mirror.

Stores with thirty cash registers
should have more than two open lanes.

Even if you win the rat race, you're still a rat.

Good enough is just good enough.

Happiness lies in our own backyard,
but it may very well be hidden by crabgrass.

No man has ever been shot doing the dishes.

I have my best ideas in the shower.

Common sense is no longer common.

Being polite has become so rare
that it's often mistaken for flirting.

We never really grow up;
we only learn how to act in public.

Life doesn't have a do-over.

A closed mouth gathers no feet.

As cell phones become thinner and smarter,
their owners do the opposite.

We all have the ability to light up a room.
Some when we enter,
some when we leave.

Dying is easy.
Comedy is hard.

A day without sunshine is like night.

A person who aims at nothing is sure to hit it.

A single fact can spoil a good argument.

If you think you might be
addicted to the hokey-pokey,
it's time to turn yourself around.

Doing nothing is difficult
because you never know when you're finished.

No man knows less
than the man who knows it all.

Bald guys never have a bad hair day.

You may need to get lost
before you really find your way.

If nothing is going your way,
you may be in the wrong lane.

You can save a place in line for one—
or maybe two—friends,
but you can't save a place in line for three.

Drive like there's a cop
around the next corner.

Nostalgia isn't what it used to be.

Breakfast may not be
the most important meal of the day.

**Without free speech
both the speaker and the hearer lose out.**

You can't have a positive life
with a negative attitude.

HEARTWARMING LIFEOLOGY

You have an entire lifetime to work,
but there's only one summer
when you're twelve years old.

Everyone has at least one story worth telling.

When a two-year-old hands you
a toy telephone you only have one choice:
to say hello.

**To win in tennis and in life,
learn to serve well.**

A smile means the same thing in every language.

**A smile is the shortest difference
between two people.**

You don't love a woman
because she is beautiful;
she is beautiful
because you love her.

Never look down at a person
unless you're helping them up.

Silent company is often more healing
than words of advice.

Today is a good day to have a good day.

To get the best out of others,
give the best of yourself.

INSPIRATIONAL LIFEOLOGY

To experience light
there must first be darkness.

Confession is good for the soul.

The Word works.

God does not ask about our ability,
but our availability.

John Bunyan wrote *The Pilgrim's Progress* in jail.

Martin Luther translated the Bible
while confined in a castle.

God has placed eternity into every heart.

The wonderful thing about adversity
is how it drives us to our knees.

If you don't tell your story,
God doesn't get the glory.

If you find yourself farther from God today
than yesterday, guess who moved?

There will be no crown bearers in heaven
who are not cross bearers on earth.

God's retirement plan is out of this world.

When you were born, you were crying
and everyone around you was smiling.
Live your life so that when you die,
you're smiling and everyone around you is crying.

INSPIRATIONAL LIFEOLOGY

Life doesn't get easier—
you just get stronger.

Backbone beats wishbone every time.

To befuddle an atheist, serve him a fine meal,
then ask him if he believes there is a cook.

Do not ask the Lord to guide your footsteps
if you are not willing to move your feet.

You cannot change your past;
you can only change your future.

Dreams worth dreaming
should be a little scary.

Life is an election in which God votes for you,
Satan votes against you,
and you cast the deciding vote.

Courage is not the absence of fear,
but the conquest of it.

One man plus God makes a majority.

The smallest good deed
is better than the grandest intention.

You cannot outgive God.

An unopened gift may as well be an empty box.

To fear death is to misunderstand life.

THOUGHT-PROVOKING
LIFEOLOGY

We whine about pedaling up the hill,
but we still expect to coast on the way down.

We fear what we don't understand.

People don't fail—they give up.

**If you agreed with everyone
no one would be right.**

Truth and reality
will always find each other eventually.

The way up and the way down are often the same.

If the only tool you have is a hammer,
every problem begins to look like a nail.

The nail that sticks up will be hammered down.

It's not possible to step into the same river twice.

The apple seemed like a good choice to Eve.

A turtle makes progress when he sticks his neck out.

The glass isn't half full or half empty;
it's just twice as big as it needs to be.

If you don't care where you're going
any road will get you there.

Freedom requires responsibility.

Responsibility requires freedom.

THOUGHT-PROVOKING LIFEOLOGY

If you start now, you won't have to run to catch up.

When science finally locates the
center of the universe, some people
will be surprised to learn they're not it.

Visionaries look at stumbling blocks
and see stepping stones.

The more you know, the less you need to show.

Truth fears no questions.

Never worry about tomorrow,
it's already tomorrow in Australia.

The ocean would be much deeper
if it didn't have so many sponges.

Everything is either ice cream or not ice cream.

Experience is what causes a person
to make new mistakes instead of old ones.

You won't find the silver lining until you look for it.

There are truths.
For example, two plus two does equal four.

The fire which warms you at a distance
will burn you when near.

Only dead fish go with the flow.

Home is the place where we are treated the best,
but grumble the most.

Airplanes take off against the wind.

Our hopes are but memories reversed.

If you hit the target every time,
the target is too big.

One day your parents put you down
and never picked you up again.

No decision is the same as a decision.

Most men would rather do nothing
than do it wrong.

Only the lead dog gets a change of scenery.

Don't panic if you're choking on an ice cube.

LIFEOLOGY
YOU ALREADY KNEW

If you play with fire, you'll get burned.

Smoking is not a good choice.

If it walks like a duck and quacks like a duck …
it's a duck.

Television is often a waste of time.

Water takes the path of least resistance.

Someday is not a day of the week.

The only time the word incorrectly isn't spelled
incorrectly is when it's spelled incorrectly.

It is no great feat to travel a smooth road.

Even a stopped clock is right twice a day.

There are things on the Internet
no one should see.

A dollar is thinner than a dime.

Appliances work better when you plug them in.

A half truth is a whole lie.

Ignorance of the law is no excuse.

No pain, no gain.

Sometimes you are going to have to do things
you don't want to do.

Honesty lightens your load.

There is no right way to do the wrong thing.

When all else fails, read the instructions.

Practice makes better.

You can't plow a field
by turning it over in your mind.

You can't push a rope.

Everyone makes mistakes.

Secrets don't keep.

Use of alcohol impairs decision-making.

There's no such thing as a free lunch.

What goes around comes around.

Anyone stuck in traffic is traffic.

Remote controls do not work more efficiently
by pushing the buttons harder.

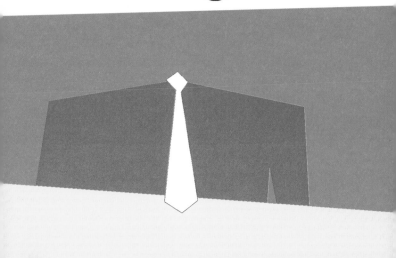

AMUSING-FACT
LIFE OLOGY

After a challenge by his editor, Dr. Seuss wrote *Green Eggs and Ham* using exactly fifty different words.

Maine is the closest US state to Africa.

The first product to have a barcode was Wrigley's Juicy Fruit gum.

Venus is the only planet to rotate clockwise.

You will always find something in the last place you look.

Mozart wrote his first opera at the age of twelve.

Cats cannot be baptized.

"The Alphabet Song," "Twinkle, Twinkle Little Star," and "Baa, Baa Black Sheep" all use the same tune.

A smile takes only thirteen muscles, a frown takes sixty-four.

The Empire State building is hit by lightning an average of twenty-three times per year.

The best thing on a basketball court is a wrestling mat.

Three words are the same in every language: *Huh*, *Hallelujah*, and *Coca-Cola*.

Lou Gehrig was the first athlete to appear on a Wheaties box.

Camels have three eyelids.

Nowhere in the nursery rhyme *Humpty Dumpty* does it say that Humpty Dumpty is an egg.

The correct name of the # symbol—commonly known as pound, number, or hashtag—is octothorpe.

Bats are not blind.

Bulls are colorblind.

Six weeks after Roger Bannister did the impossible by breaking the four-minute mile, John Landy broke Bannister's record by 1.5 seconds.

A typical golf ball has 336 dimples.

A nanosecond is a billionth of a second.

Armadillos almost always
give birth to quadruplets.

It takes eight minutes and twenty seconds
for light from the sun to reach the Earth.

The wingspan of a 747 is longer than
the Wright brothers' first flight.

At the time the current oldest person
on Earth was born, there was a completely
different set of human beings on the planet.

Manhole covers are round so they
don't fall down the hole when tilted sideways.

During his lifetime,
Vincent van Gogh sold one painting.

PERSPICACIOUS LIFEOLOGY

Life is not something you watch
but something you do.

Even if there is no vision, tomorrow still lies ahead.

Hope for the best, prepare for the worst.

**Learn from the mistakes of others.
You can't live long enough to make them all yourself.**

No person is above any job.

Knowledge is power.

If you enjoy the fruit, pluck not the flower.

A guilty conscience needs no accuser.

Those who run from danger
are not lacking in courage,
they're exhibiting wisdom.

What we learn after we think we know it all
makes all the difference.

Trouble brings experience,
and experience brings wisdom.

Don't give up athanasia
chasing something evanescent.

You don't write because you want to say something;
you write because you've got something to say.

Sometimes you won't get closure
and you just have to move on.

PERSPICACIOUS LIFEOLOGY

Neither success nor failure is necessarily final.

Be the kind of person your dog thinks you are.

Don't look back unless your desire is to turn back.

Don't let yesterday use up too much of today.

Many an opportunity is lost
because a man is out looking for four-leaf clovers.

Everything in moderation—including moderation.

The one who complains about the way the ball
bounces is likely the one who dropped it.

The best response to anger is silence.

Nobody trips over mountains.
It is the pebble that causes you to stumble.

Life would be so much easier
if everyone read the manual.

Sometimes the best thing to say is nothing.

Diplomacy is thinking twice before saying nothing.

Lead, follow, or get out of the way.

To win at chess, attack the king.

Regrets tend to come from things you didn't do,
not things you did do.

COMFORTING
LIFEOLOGY

Not everything depends on you.

The best is yet to come.

God's mercy is greater than
your brokenness.

Comparison is the thief of joy.

It's okay to cry.

No one has it all figured out.

Happiness is not the absence of problems
but the wisdom to know they will not last.

Most people in the world
would love to have your bad days.

There's a bit of irony in the idea that
one of the secrets to self-empowerment
is realizing you don't have to go it alone.

If you're uncomfortable, God will bring you comfort.
But if you're getting too comfortable,
God will make you uncomfortable.

If you focus only on what's tearing you apart,
you forget what's holding you together.

Broken crayons still color.

When a crayon breaks, two can color.

If you can laugh at it, you can live with it.

When you're burdened by how far you have to go,
turn around and see how far you've come.

Failure is the best teacher.

If you survive a really bad decision,
chances are you at least have a really good story.

Some of the best days of your life
have not yet happened.

Everything will be okay in the end.
If it's not okay, it's not the end.

UNEXPECTED LIFEOLOGY

The early bird may get the worm,
but the second mouse gets the cheese.

The light at the end of the tunnel
is sometimes an oncoming freight train.

Before you criticize someone, walk a mile in their
shoes. That way, you'll be too far away for them to
hear you. And you'll have their shoes.

When it comes to giving,
some people stop at nothing.

On the other hand are different fingers.

A job done right need never be done again.
Except mowing the lawn.

Triumph is merely try with a little added umph.

Thou shalt not steal.
The government hates competition.

Change is good, but dollars are better.

Only Robinson Crusoe had everything done by Friday.

**He who hesitates is not only lost,
but miles from the next exit.**

To make any dream come true, wake up and work.

A hangover is the wrath of grapes.

If the clerk gives you too much change, give it back.
The confused look on their face
is worth every penny.

UNEXPECTED LIFEOLOGY

One thing that never changes
is constant change.

If you can't remember how to throw a boomerang,
just wait. It'll come back to you.

He who laughs last probably just didn't get the joke.

Frogs have it easy—they can eat what bugs them.

Children must always wear a seatbelt,
unless there are fifty of them in a single yellow vehicle.

You never know what you really have
until you clean your room.

Change is inevitable,
except from a vending machine.

You can teach a middle-age dog new tricks.

**Two wrongs don't make a right,
but two Wrights make an airplane.**

Don't judge a book by its movie.

Better late than really late.

If you're caught in the mousetrap,
go ahead and eat the cheese.

Be yourself because everyone else is already taken.

Eagles may soar,
but weasels don't get sucked into jet engines.

UNEXPECTED LIFEOLOGY

To make headlines, sleep on corduroy pillows.

A man who keeps cutting corners
will find himself going in circles.

A bicycle can't stand up by itself
because it is two tired.

Some days you win, some days you learn.

It's always darkest before the dawn.
So if you're going to steal the neighbor's newspaper,
that's the time to do it.

History is a great teacher.
Unfortunately, it's old news.

Keep your temper; no one else wants it.

Keep your words sweet,
just in case you have to eat them.

**Never put off until tomorrow
what you can get somebody else to do today.**

Time flies like an arrow.
Fruit flies like a banana.

**Instead of complaining about the dog-days
of summer, be grateful you're not a fire hydrant.**

Be true to your teeth, or they'll be false to you.

Nobody likes change, except a wet baby.

Every journey begins by changing shoes.

FRIENDLY-REMINDER LIFEOLOGY

You will become like the people you hang out with.

You do not need a parachute to skydive.
You definitely need a parachute to skydive twice.

"I had no choice" is never a valid excuse.

Attitude determines altitude.

Some days you're the pigeon
and some days you're the statue.

God moves in mysterious ways.

When packing for a vacation,
take half as much clothing and twice as much money.

A mousetrap always provides free cheese.

It's never too late to start over.

Never leave hold of what you've got
until you've got hold of something else.

Never play poker with someone named Doc or Ace.

A good place to start is where you are.

The grass may be greener on the other side of the
fence, but you still have to mow it.

If nothing ever changed, there'd be no butterflies.

Good habits are formed; bad habits we fall into.

Once you make your point, stop talking.

The Ten Commandments are not multiple choice.

If you are praised lavishly,
enjoy the taste but don't swallow it whole.

You can't fix yourself by breaking someone else.

Do not regret growing older.
It is a privilege denied to many.

The best throw with the dice is to throw them away.

Get mad and you'll never get anything else.

Character is built through many acts,
but may be lost by a single one.

Ideas won't work unless you do.

Opportunity may knock only once,
but temptation leans on the doorbell.

The best angle from which to approach any problem
is the Try-angle.

Hope is a good thing,
but not if you depend on it solely.

Age doesn't measure maturity.

The check is probably not in the mail.

The great benefit of experience is
how it enables you to recognize a mistake
when you make it again.

Speak well of your enemies ... you made them.

No matter where your journey leads,
you will never find the girl who smiles out at you
from the travel brochure.

Confidence is the feeling you have
before you fully understand the situation.

Honesty is still the best policy.

What you don't know can hurt you
(e.g. the location of snakes, snipers, snowbanks,
and snapping turtles).

Never test the depth of the water with both feet.

If you chase two rabbits, both will escape.

A groundless rumor often covers a lot of ground.

Don't insult the alligator
until after you've crossed the river.

Those who never walk except where they see footprints
will make no discoveries.

When you point your finger at someone,
three fingers are pointing back at you.

You shouldn't expect to get everything right
the first time.

Don't lend what you can't afford to lose.

Talk is cheap.

Never ask a barber if you need a haircut.

The sooner you fall behind,
the more time you'll have to catch up.

You can pick your friends and you can pick your nose,
but you can't pick your friend's nose.

It's never wrong to do the right thing.

Choose your battles. You can't fight them all.
You can't win them all.

If *you* don't say it, *they* can't repeat it.

If you don't want anyone to read it, see it, or hear it,
don't write it, send it, or say it.

The best way to get along is to go along.

The worst way to innovate is to go along.

If you can't take the heat, get out of the kitchen.

Never play leapfrog with a unicorn.

Words have meaning.

To move forward you may first need to
move sideways or even backwards.

**Change is not reform,
any more than noise is music.**

The lesser of two evils is still evil.

The quieter you are, the more you will hear.

First things first.

Going to church doesn't make you a Christian any more than standing in a garage makes you a car.

If you're about to take a sharp turn, slow down.

A smile is your personal welcome mat.

Half the people in the world are below average.

He who dies with the most toys still dies.

If you've chosen to be unconventional, cherish the scorn you've invited.

POSSIBLY ERRONEOUS LIFE⊙LOGY

History repeats itself.

No good deed goes unpunished.

Some days it doesn't pay to get outta bed.

Never blame society.

127 percent of all people exaggerate.

42.7 percent of all statistics are made up on the spot.

If it's too loud, you're too old.

If it moves and shouldn't, duct tape it.
If it doesn't move and should, WD-40 it.

The wheel that squeaks loudest
is first to be replaced.

The world is run by C students.

Better to have and not need
than to need and not have.

It's easier to apologize than ask permission.

You may have to kiss a lot of toads
before you find your prince.

**The most expensive wedding
usually ends with the quickest divorce.**

Every bad thing done on the face of the earth has
been done by man—but so has every good thing.

POSSIBLY ERRONEOUS LIFEOLOGY

Laugh at what people do,
not at what they are.

To steal ideas from one person is plagiarism,
to steal ideas from many is research.

Great minds think alike.

The future is not what it used to be.

It matters not whether you win or lose;
what matters is whether I win or lose.

Very few problems today
are still problems tomorrow.

The other line always moves faster.

GRAMMAR
LIFEOLOGY

Eliminate commas, that are, not necessary.

Minimize the use of exclamation points!!!

It is wrong to ever split an infinitive.

No sentence fragments.

Use apostrophe's correctly.

**Never use run-on sentences they have
to include punctuation.**

And never begin a sentence with
a conjunction like because, but, and, or however.

Verbs has to agree with their subject.

Never use a preposition to end a sentence with.

Avoid clichés like the plague.

Never use no double negatives.

Proofread carefully to see if you any words out.

I before E—except after C
or when you happen to be planning
a feisty heist on a weird beige foreign neighbor.

WORKSHOP
LIFEOLOGY

Measure twice, cut once.

Let the saw do the work.

Righty tighty, lefty loosey.

Sand with the grain.

On a table saw, cut plywood best face up.

With a circular saw, cut plywood best face down.

**If building in the summer,
allow for winter shrinkage.**

If building in the winter,
allow for summer expansion.

Disconnect the power before changing the blade.

Allow for kerf.
(That's the space left after a saw blade makes its cut.)

Wood is weak across the grain
but strong with the grain.

Dull tools are more dangerous than sharp tools.

Don't use your favorite screwdriver or chisel
to open paint cans.

TWO-WORD LIFEOLOGY

Play nice.

Seasons change.

Live large.

Be yourself.

Be honest.

Sex sells.

Try again.

Live grudgeless.

Share ideas.

Help others.

Stay positive.

Never quit.

Do good.

Delay gratification.

Eschew obfuscation.

Look up.

Dream dreams.

Work hard.

Serve soup.

Don't settle.

Don't litter.

Life happens.

Seek truth.

Pursue God.

Dig deep.

Wash hands.

Give thanks.

Be determined.

Make memories.

Hug longer.

Procrastinate tomorrow.

Carpe diem.

Share success.

Give credit.

Choose joy.

Count blessings.

Love wins.

LIFEOLOGY
FOR PARENTS

Ignore the stickball dents on the garage door.

If it's important to your kids,
it should be important to you.

One of the great privileges reserved for fathers
is that when we look at our own children, we get
just a small sampling of God's love for each of us.

A kid spells love T-I-M-E.

Wake your kid for a lunar eclipse.

Rescue your children at the top of any slippery slope.

Babies are born small so you can hold them.
A lot.

Quit smoking.

Give noogies.

Let kids be kids.

Mom and Dad should kiss in the kitchen.

Kids live up or down to their parents' expectations.

It's impossible to spoil a newborn.

Remember what you were like
when you were sixteen.

Children need more models and fewer critics.

Don't miss your kids.
After they move out there will be plenty of time
to re-sod, re-paint, re-screen, re-carpet, and relax.

Children may leave home, but their stuff will be in
your attic or basement forever.

It's much easier to get your kids on the right track
before they learn to outsmart you.

Never forget that your kids will choose
your nursing home.

Sometimes parents forget that our ultimate
goal is to make ourselves obsolete—
to work our way out of a job.

A truly rich man is one whose children
run into his arms when his hands are empty.

A food your seven-year-old gags on
will be her favorite as an adult.

Band-Aids® make most boo-boos better.

The best way to train up a child
in the way he should go
is to travel that way yourself.

It's impossible to spoon feed a baby
without also opening your own mouth.

The best thing a dad can do for his kids
is love their mother.

The best thing to spend on your children
is time.

Some men live yearning
for a blessing from their father.
Other men live empowered
by a blessing from their father.

The child you punish for not playing nice
was probably provoked
by the innocent-looking sibling.

Stop and catch the fireflies.

The goal is to live long enough
to be a burden to your children.

The best way to help single mothers
is to create fewer of them.

When your kids hit bottom, don't pile on.

Kids are future adults.

Your children will follow your footsteps easier
than they follow your advice.

Children need moms and dads.

Children are a gift.
Accept that gift.

Even if a son or daughter turns their back on you,
don't turn your back on them.

Your heritage cannot be altered,
your legacy is still being written.

LIFEOLOGY
FOR KIDS

You can't hide a piece of broccoli in a glass of milk.

If you take turns, everyone gets a turn.

I'm rubber and you're glue.
Whatever you say bounces off me and sticks to you.

When you share, you get more.

Read.

Unplug.

Cheaters never prosper.

At the supermarket, you get *one* treat.

Learn the ten-second tidy.

Don't throw sand.

Chew with your mouth closed.

**When Mom says you climbed too high,
you're probably still safe. But when Dad says
you climbed too high, you climbed too high.**

Your mom and dad were kids once.
Really.

Say please and thank you.

Don't put nickels, Legos®, lima beans,
or Junior Mints® up your nose.

Today is not your birthday. (Unless it is.)

Home is where your mom is.

When trading baseball cards,
the best deals are good for both sides.

Baby brothers and sisters don't steal
your parents' love—they multiply it.

Never pet a strange dog.

You really don't have to listen to your parents
until they start counting.

If you want a puppy,
start by asking for a pony.

GOOD-TO-KNOW
LIFEOLOGY

Don't wear polka-dot underwear
under white shorts.

Cotton is more comfy than polyester.

If you can't beat your computer at chess,
try kickboxing.

You can't fix a kinked Slinky®.

When a made-for-TV movie asks,
What's the true meaning of Christmas?
they never get it right.

An hour spent in the library
is worth a month in the laboratory.

Choose a neighborhood
where people wave from their front yard.

It typically takes a long time
to find a shorter way.

Evil exists.
But it typically comes in disguise.

CONTRADICTORY LIFEOLOGY

Opposites attract.

Birds of a feather flock together.

Two heads are better than one.

Too many cooks spoil the broth.

The more, the merrier.

Two's company, three's a crowd.

Out of sight, out of mind.

Absence makes the heart grow fonder.

Nothing ventured, nothing gained.

Better safe than sorry.

Time is money.

Money talks.

Talk is cheap.

You can't judge a book by its cover.

Clothes make the man.

Haste makes waste.

He who hesitates is lost.

Actions speak louder than words.

The pen is mightier than the sword.

The bigger, the better.

Good things come in small packages.

Look before you leap.

Leap and the net will appear.

Hitch your wagon to a star.

Don't bite off more than you can chew.

An eye for an eye.

Turn the other cheek.

All for one and one for all.

Every man for himself.

CONTRADICTORY LIFEOLOGY

ONE-WORD LIFEOLOGY

Read.

Believe.

Smile.

Sleep.

Dream.

Wonder.

Wander.

Scripture.

Hope.

Apologize.

Bacon.

Chocolate.

Lead.

Create.

Doubt.

Ask.

Question.

Sacrifice.

Surrender.

Play.

Love.

Hug.

LIFE☉L☉GY
FROM SCRIPTURE

The truth will set you free.
(John 8:32 NIV)

The love of money is the root of all kinds of evil.
(1 Timothy 6:10 NLT)

Weeping may last through the night,
but joy comes with the morning.
(Psalm 30:5 NLT)

Don't let your left hand know
what your right hand is doing.
(Matthew 6:3 NLT)

Let not the sun go down upon your wrath.
(Ephesians 4:26)

Cast thy bread upon the waters.
(Ecclesiastes 11:1)

Give not that which is holy unto the dogs,
neither cast ye your pearls before swine.
(Matthew 7:6)

They that seek the Lord
shall not lack any good thing.
(Psalm 34:10)

No one can serve two masters.
(Matthew 6:24)

Don't just listen to God's word.
You must do what it says.
(James 1:22 NLT)

A fool uttereth all his mind:
but a wise man keepeth it in till afterwards.
(Proverbs 29:11)

A cheerful heart is good medicine.
(Proverbs 17:22 NIV)

Everything is possible for one who believes.
(Mark 9:23 NIV)

The heart is deceitful above all things.
(Jeremiah 17:9)

Those who use the sword will die by the sword.
(Matthew 26:52 NLT)

From everyone who has been given much,
much will be demanded.
(Luke 12:48 NIV)

Those unwilling to work will not get to eat.
(2 Thessalonians 3:10 NLT)

Hatred stirs up conflict,
but love covers over all wrongs.
(Proverbs 10:12 NIV)

Give, and it will be given to you.
(Luke 6:39 NIV)

Whatever your hand finds to do,
do it with all your might.
(Ecclesiastes 9:10 NIV)

Whatsoever a man soweth,
that shall he also reap.
(Galatians 6:7)

Man shall not live by bread alone.
(Luke 4:4)

The fear of the Lord
is the beginning of knowledge.
(Proverbs 1:7)

There is no fear in love.
(1 John 4:18)

Keep on knocking,
and the door will be opened to you.
(Matthew 7:7 NLT)

Do not be conformed
to the pattern of this world.
(Romans 12:2 NIV)

LIFEOLOGY
FROM SHAKESPEARE

All that glitters is not gold.

Men of few words are the best men.

Virtue is beauty.

To thine own self be true.

Uneasy lies the head that wears the crown.

It is a wise father that knows his own child.

Neither a borrower nor a lender be.

The course of true love never did run smooth.

It is one thing to be tempted, another thing to fall.

Be not afraid of greatness.

Smooth runs the water where the brook is deep.

In friendship, as in love, we are often happier
through our ignorance than our knowledge.

Men are men; the best sometimes forget.

How sharper than a serpent's tooth
it is to have a thankless child!

All the world's a stage,
and all the men and women merely players.

A man may fish with the worm that hath eat of a king,
and eat of the fish that hath fed of that worm.

LIFEOLOGY FROM SHAKESPEARE

Society is no comfort to one not sociable.

If music be the food of love, play on.

Oppose not rage while rage is in its force, but give it way awhile and let it waste.

Every one can master a grief but he that has it.

There is a history in all men's lives.

Lord, what fools these mortals be.

Trust not him that hath once broken faith.

Some are born great, some achieve greatness, and some have greatness thrust upon them.

Few love to hear the sins they love to act.

Time is the king of men; he is both their parent, and he is their grave, and gives them what he will, not what they crave.

An old man is twice a child.

'Tis no sin for a man to labor in his vocation.

God on our side, doubt not of victory.

There's a time for all things.

When great leaves fall, the winter is at hand.

There's place and means for every man alive.

LIFEOLOGY FROM SHAKESPEARE

With eager feeding food doth choke the feeder.

If I lose mine honor, I lose myself.

The fool doth think he is wise.

What is the city but the people?

Brevity is the soul of wit.

With mirth and laughter let old wrinkles come.

The first thing we do, let's kill all the lawyers.

**When devils will the blackest sins put on,
they do suggest at first with heavenly shows.**

There is many a man hath more hair than wit.

The nature of bad news infects the teller.

The better part of valor is discretion.

Death, as the psalmist saith,
is certain to all; all shall die.

Wisdom and goodness to the vile seem vile.

Suspicion always haunts the guilty mind;
The thief doth fear each bush an officer.

**We know what we are,
but know not what we may be.**

Love all, trust a few, do wrong to none.

LIFEOLOGY FROM SHAKESPEARE

CAREER-POLITICIAN LIFE⊙LOGY

I will not raise taxes.

I am not a criminal.

Free college for everyone!

My marriage is solid as a rock.

My administration will be open and transparent.

You can trust me.

That quote was taken out of context.

I'm resigning from office
to spend more time with my family.

CLASSIC LIFEOLOGY

You can't make an omelet
without breaking a few eggs.

The squeaky wheel gets the grease.

If it is to be, it is up to me.

Give a man a fish, and you feed him for a day.
Teach a man to fish
and you feed him for a lifetime.

A chain is only as strong as its weakest link.

A picture is worth a thousand words.

A coward dies a thousand deaths,
the brave just once.

Trust in God but keep your powder dry.

There's safety in numbers.

Necessity is the mother of invention.

You can't judge a book by its cover.

You catch more flies with honey
than with vinegar.

Beggars can't be choosers.

It's always darkest just before the dawn.

An idle mind is the devil's playground.

A bird in the hand
is worth two in the bush.

Honesty is the best policy.

Red sky at night, sailors delight.
Red sky in morning, sailor take warning.

Don't believe everything you hear.

Rome wasn't built in a day.

Hard work never killed anybody.

Still waters run deep.

It ain't over til the fat lady sings.

Every dog has its day.

The apple never falls far from the tree.

It's not whether you win or lose,
but how you play the game.

NEW CLASSIC
LIFEOLOGY

The only place you find success before work
is in the dictionary.

Dance like no one's going to put it on YouTube.

You miss 100 percent of the shots you don't take.

Let Nigerian princes lie.

Practice—and Photoshop—makes perfect.

If you don't stand for something,
you will fall for anything.

Garbage in, garbage out.

You fail only when you stop trying.

Pain is weakness leaving the body.

What doesn't kill you makes you stronger.

Don't do the crime if you can't do the time.

Do what you love
and you'll never work a day in your life.

You snooze, you lose.

A camel is a horse designed by a committee.

If the grass is greener on the other side of the fence,
it's because they take better care of it.

One man's trash is another man's treasure.

Ask me no questions, I'll tell you no lies.

NEW CLASSIC LIFEOLOGY

Despite the high cost of living,
it remains a popular item.

If you're not part of the solution,
you're part of the problem.

Keep your friends close and your enemies closer.

If it ain't broke, don't fix it.

Today is the first day of the rest of your life.

You can't make an omelet without posting a few pics.

A journey of a thousand sites
begins with a single click.

MURPHY'S LIFEOLOGY

Anything that can go wrong, will go wrong.

Left to themselves,
things tend to go from bad to worse.

Nature always sides with the hidden flaw.

A verbal contract is not worth
the paper it's printed on.

Buttered bread falls to the floor
butter side down.

If everything seems to be going well, you have
obviously overlooked something.

The bag that gets dropped
is the one with the eggs.

The end user does not know what he wants
until he sees what he gets.

Generalities are generally false.

Count on appliances to break down
within a week after the warranty expires.

After reassembling,
there will always be one part left over.

If the shoe fits, it's ugly.

The most efficient way to discover typos in e-mails
is to click Send.

If at first you don't succeed,
destroy all evidence that you tried.

Whenever you set out to do something,
something else has to be done first.

Everything costs more and takes longer
than you think.

It is impossible to make anything foolproof
because fools are so ingenious.

BUSINESS LIFE☺LOGY

Perception is reality.

The longer the title, the less important the job.

People don't value what they get for free.

Overhead can't turn a profit.

Plan B distracts from Plan A.

Stagnancy is suicide.

Take calculated risks.

Before you purchase that stock everyone is buying,
find out why the sellers are selling.

Surround yourself with good people.

The only meetings that start on time
are the ones you're late for.

You're not selling stuff,
you're selling experiences.

The customer is always right.

Never bring a problem to your boss
unless you present a solution at the same time.

It is much harder to find a job
than to keep one.

Flaunt your brand.

Expense accounts that end in .00
are more likely to draw suspicion.

A vacation should be just long enough that
your boss misses you, but not long enough to
discover how well they can get along without you.

The volume of paper expands
to fill the available briefcase.

If you don't take care of the customer,
somebody else will.

One man's red tape
is another man's treasured procedural.

People will buy anything
that's one to a customer.

If you tell the boss you were late for work
because you had a flat tire, the next morning
you will have a flat tire.

The trouble with most self-made men
is they tend to worship their creator.

Work expands to fit the time allotted for it.

Identifying a scapegoat
does not solve the problem.

Do what you do well.
Don't do what you don't do well.

Failure is part of the process.

The person who tells the world about the better mousetrap will have more success than the person who builds the better mousetrap.

Ask for help.

Location, location, location.

There's no such thing as bad publicity.

If you're irreplaceable,
you'll never be promoted.

NEW PERSPECTIVE
LIFEOLOGY

If you think you have it tough,
you need to read more history books.

There are so many ways to die,
it's a miracle anyone's alive.

An intelligent mind is never bored.

If something is worth doing, it's worth doing well.

If you pose for too many pictures,
the world will pass you by.

One day, when your life finally flashes before your eyes,
make sure it's worth watching.

Crises bring out the best in the best of us,
and the worst in the worst of us.

Only a fool knows everything.
A wise man knows how little he knows.

The first to apologize is the bravest.
The first to forgive is the strongest.
The first to forget is the happiest.

Do what's right, not what's easy.

Everyone is a self-made person,
but only the successful admit it.

You can't do anything if you don't show up.

A good plan today
is better than a perfect plan tomorrow.

If you've made up your mind you can do something,
you're absolutely right.

If you've made up your mind you can't do something,
you're absolutely right.

You are unique.

Good judgment comes from experience.
Experience comes from poor judgment.

We cannot direct the wind
but we can adjust the sails.

Be more concerned about what your
conscience whispers than what other people shout.

Days may drag by but years fly by.

The only person worth envying
is the person who doesn't envy.

Happiness will never come to those who fail
to appreciate what they already have.

Live every day as if it were your last
and some day you'll be right.

Blowing out someone else's candle
won't make yours shine any brighter.

When you draw a line in the sand,
make sure you're on the right side.

You cannot be held responsible for all the things
that happen to you, but you are responsible
for the way you act when they happen.

NEW PERSPECTIVE LIFEOLOGY

Worrying will not take away tomorrow's troubles.
But it does take away today's peace.

Some people get angry because
God put thorns on roses, while others praise him
for putting roses among thorns.

A good exercise for the heart
is to bend down and help another up.

Success is the first attempt after the final failure.

Courage is knowing what not to fear.

The real measure of your wealth is how much
you'd be worth if you lost all your money.

The purpose in life is to give away your gift.

A good scare can be even more valuable
than good advice.

A bird sitting in a tree is never afraid
of the branch breaking because its trust
is not in the branch, but in its own wings.

It is never too late
to do something you've always wanted to do.

If you eat a live toad in the morning, nothing worse
will happen to you for the rest of the day.

One may travel the world
in search of a worthy adventure
and find it only when you return home.

ABOUT THE AUTHOR

Prior to becoming a full-time author and speaker, Jay Payleitner served as a freelance radio producer for a bevy of international movements, including the Salvation Army, Prison Fellowship, Bible League, Voice of the Martyrs, and National Center for Fathering.

As a family advocate, life pundit, and humorist, Jay has sold some half-million books, including *52 Things Kids Need from a Dad* and *What If God Wrote Your Bucket List?* His books have been translated into French, German, Spanish, and Russian.

Jay and his high school sweetheart, Rita, live in the Chicago area where they raised five great kids, loved on ten foster babies, and are cherishing grandparenthood.

There's much more at jaypayleitner.com.